i

Wicked Dew

By Steve Russell

Winner of the Poetry First Book Award
Native Writers Circle of the Americas
2008

Published by Dog Iron Press

127 Blazing Star Drive
Georgetown, Texas 78633-9995

Dedicated to my family in the Indian sense, the survivors.

Wa do.

ACKNOWLEDGEMENTS:

"Repatriation" first appeared in *Moccasin Telegraph,* Vol. 4, No. 6 (1996).

"The Year They Drilled for Oil," "Eleven Mile Hill," and "Bison Bones" first appeared in *South Dakota Review,* Vol. 38, No. 1 (2000).

"Donna's Potsherds," "How to Succeed as an Indian Poet," and "Chitto Harjo" first appeared in *Messenger Journal of Cherokee Literature,* Vol. 1, No. 1 (2001).

"What Indians Want" first appeared in *Gatherings: The En'owkin Journal of First North American Peoples*, Vol. 13, 81-82 (2002).

"Disruption, Spring 1997" first appeared in *Hypatia: A Journal of Feminist Philosophy*, Vol.18, No.2 (2003).

"Indistinguishable Color" first appeared in *Coloring Book: An Eclectic Anthology of Fiction and Poetry by Multicultural Writers* (boice-Terrel Allen, ed., 2003).

"Dreaming" first appeared in *Cream City Review*, Vol. 27, No. 1 (2003).

"To My Grandfather," "Not Juan Valdez," "Young Warrior," "At the Vietnam Veterans' Memorial," and "Seeing Off the Troop Train" first appeared in *Genocide of the Mind* (Marijo Moore, ed., 2003).

"Honor Rap" first appeared in *Pulse* (Heartsounds Press, May 4, 2004).

"Indian America," "Blood Quantum," "Chitto Harjo," "What I Learned and Didn't Learn at the Bristow, Oklahoma Historical Society Museum," and "Bosque Redondo: Homage to Yevgeny Yevtushenko" first appeared in *Sequoyah Rising* (Carolina Academic Press, 2010).

TABLE OF CONTENTS

As wicked dew as e'er my mother brush'd
With raven's feather. . .

The Tempest, Act I, Scene II

To My Grandfather
                    for Judson George Russell

I.

I told him I wanted to be like Mickey Mantle,
who escaped the poverty of rural Oklahoma,
and appeared to own New York,
a grand place located near Oz.

Mickey Mantle got to play in the World Series every
year,
which I took to be annual games
between the New York Yankees and the Brooklyn
Dodgers
to determine possession of New York.

"What position do you want to play?"
"Just like Mickey Mantle. Batter!"

Grampa laughed and laughed
until the laughs found the smoke in his lungs
and turned to coughs.

II.

Grampa always wore a suit and tie to town.

He would walk to the post office, check Box 384, and head for the Playmor pool hall. This was a men's place and Granma did not approve.

It was cool and dark. If I was with Grampa, and if I was quiet, I could watch the elders play dominoes around cigarette-burned tables with brass spitoons at the corners.

I often lost track of who won among the tall stories of the oil boom days and it took a long time for me to realize that the elders lost track of who won, too.

I learned to play dominoes and to lose track of who won at Grampa's elbow, sipping my Grapette, uninterested in the stink of his Falstaff, and oblivious to the clouds from his Pall Malls.

Once or twice I tried to come into the Playmor without Grampa, but they always chased me off.

III.

When I was fifteen
and at home alone,
my Aunt Eleanor called
to tell me that Grampa was right,
he would not be coming home from the VA Hospital in
Muscogee.

I raged.
I fought with myself over whether to follow him.

The old Scots-Irish roughneck came to me in the Indian
way
and told me gently that I had work to do
and my grandmother needed me
and I should hold fast like the warrior I would be.
It was not a good day to die.

Some time after the funeral
I left the public school deathtrap for good
and for once I did not hide in the public library.
I walked into the Playmor alone
in the middle of the day
and nobody chased me off.

IV.

I left Oklahoma
and as the years accumulate
Oklahoma almost leaves me.
The road home is distant and dusty and even more
unlikely
than the road here.

I have seen New York.
And Oz.
And College.

Soon I will play dominoes with my own grandchildren.

And although I still cannot tie a necktie, Grampa,
I have taken your name.

I have never held a job that did not interest me. I have
never been rich but I have never been poor.

I remember you blowing Pall Mall smoke in my ear
to soothe an earache

and how you walked an Indian child down Main Street,
not hearing that which should not be spoken,

and I want you to know

I am still playing batter.

Probably Wolf Clan

Probably Wolf Clan, so the numbers say.
From that part of the Heptagon least drowned
by the flood of European blood.

Without a Uku, we listen to the numbers,
dry as anthropologists,
hungry as the unquiet dead
of a European town.

European nomenclature, innumerate,
settles like timeless mist
on the colorless feathers of a Cherokee man,
probably Wolf Clan

Indistinguishable Color

A truckstop on the west side of Albuquerque.
Late in the day and short more than a dollar,
I pull myself aboard a muddy Kenworth
        of indistinguishable color.

The desert turns to desert,
eighteen big ones hum on I-40
as the Western sky
explores the colors
of Provider's palette.

In the mirror
Albuquerque is a scatter of glittering ore
salted around the Sandias,
spilling toward the darkening desert.

Beauty behind me.
Beauty before me.

The country music station is lost with the daylight.
Scanning the airwaves, the radio bumps against a Dine'
voice.
My benefactor punches in the station
long enough to make his point:

"Listen to that heathen shit!"
(Has he heard of the Code Talkers?)

I stare ahead where the sun has sucked all penumbral
light below the horizon leaving the desert
    of indistinguishable color.

        "I guess they gave this Godforsaken desert
to the Navajos because there's nothing out here they
could screw up."
        (We are not in Dinetah, but the wild beauty
of this land teases at the edge of the headlights' glow.)

Jaw aching, I ask to be let off in Gallup near the string of
bars and pawnshops cast along the highway to net the
Indian trade.

        "I thought you were going to Phoenix.
Well, be careful of the drunk Indians along here. Nothin'
more dangerous than a drunk Indian."

I catch my duffel, wave my goodbye, and wander among
the fullbloods on the streets of Gallup, just another
passing pilgrim

        of indistinguishable color.

Blood Quantum

Marry for love, squaw man.
Marry for love, clanless mother.

But have a care, Tsalagi,
for the thin red line, thinning to gray.

The Keetoowahs want a fourth.
The Eastern Band, like the marrow bank,
wants a sixteenth.

So have a care, Tsalagi,
for the thin red line, thinning to gray.

There is strength in numbers but also gray gone
oblivion.

Landless, clanless, without medicine or meaning,

tourist tipis and model names on trucks,

here we remember proud people

who married for love.

Donna's Potsherds

I see you in the black on gray Anasazi patterns but I
leave them on the ground to carry their message to the
ages.

I hear you in the singing crystal bowl with the velvet
sheathed wand that I passed on to Mary and she put away
safe from the hazards of grandchildren you never saw.

I touch your breast in the smooth Santa Clara glaze of the
cat we bought at Four Corners after the turtle was sold in
the time it took us to eat the fry bread.

I smell your sweat on the wind over Chaco Canyon
where we hiked the outlying trails and made love in a
sleeping bag in the back of the red Ford Explorer.

I remember you in the taste of salt water from my eyes or
from the rough seas off Galveston, scattering your ashes
as you instructed me, trying to sing "Amazing Grace"
with my voice, like everything else, broken.

Cherokee Love

There is no love in Cherokee.
No falling in or falling out,
no marry now or live in doubt,
no changing weather love in Cherokee.

There is no love in Cherokee.
No abstract love or kiss of fate,
no born too soon or born too late,
no accidental love in Cherokee.

There is no love in Cherokee,
objectless and objectified,
nominalized and sanctified.
Just subject/object intertwined,
eager noun and verb combined,
the grown together love of Cherokees.

Tracy's Pedestal

You ask me for a pedestal,
but I'll love you as an equal.
I'll love you days and love you nights
as if there'd be no sequel.
For though I'd make your pedestal
and add to it a crown,
you'd surely find the going up
not worth the coming down.
The problem, dear, with pedestals,
the truth I must confide,
is needing not to reach too far
to have you by my side.

August 30, 1994
(Married February 11, 1995)

Lust

A simple lust to own the moment
if not the woman,
as I lie here
and you lie there
and we lie here.

On the day a dam is filled
the silt begins to gather
and the bottom rises.

On the day a baby bird
breaks free to daylight
first flight
stains the future.

On the day the masterwork is made
colors fade
and deep within the canvas
yellow and brittle
begin their conquest.

So pardon me this simple lust.
I cannot own the woman,

but the moment,
as I lie here
and you lie there
and we lie here
as close as we ever shall be.

Teach Me

Teach me, White Father, so I may understand.

I understand slavery.

For the fault of their warriors, a people may have to serve another,

may feel the sting of disgrace and open themselves to the indignities

that go with serving another's will.

I do not understand chattel slavery,

the owning of human beings forever,

breeding them--this one for fighting, that one for sexual pleasure--

and locking them in a today with no tomorrows.

Teach me, White Father, so I may understand.

I understand lust.

For the raging need in a man's blood, he may pursue a
woman in dishonorable ways

especially without the proper guidance of elders.

I do not understand rape,

the taking by force,

the opening of unwilling legs,

the dry friction and brief bloody violence

locked in a today with no tomorrows.

Teach me, White Father, so I may understand.

I understand farming.

For the bounty of the earth, a man might build a fence

along the lines in his mind

and if he sets the lines on paper

come to believe they are real.

I do not understand your ways with our mother the earth

or what kind of farmer pours poison on the soil,

opens a dry gash and forces the metal-sheathed plow,

only to watch the wind scatter the soil in great clouds

that sooth our mother's wounds when the rain finally comes

but produce nothing for our children to eat,

locking them on the barren land

in a today with no tomorrows?

Teach me, White Father, so that I may understand.

Seeing Off the Troop Train

For Bessie Lois Russell

Going to war must be grand!

"Nobody elected Truman," Granma grumped, and I was too young to know she hadn't voted for Roosevelt either.

All the important people were there, and the Indians too.

I watched from Grampa's shoulders as the shiny black engine, impossibly tall, belched enough steam to rival the politicians behind their red, white and blue bunting.

"We got no business over there," Granma grumped.

Every Indian boy of age was on that platform, all dressed alike

And all the girls in town, it seemed, were pouring forth hugs, kisses and tears.

The high school band played marches, everybody cheered, and I desperately wished myself old enough and wise enough to ride the train to Korea.

Twelve years later,

I still thought going to war must be grand.

What does an Indian high school dropout in rural
Oklahoma do that is

(legal) (honorable) (sensible)?

"We got no business over there," Granma grumped,

"and nobody elected Johnson."

No band; no speeches; no steam trains.

By that time, I knew she hadn't voted for Kennedy,
either.

The train that went to Korea didn't stop in Vietnam, so
we said our goodbyes at the airport in Oklahoma City.

Twenty-eight years later, my son is a volunteer soldier.

Nobody elected Bush or his crew of 20th Century retreads.

Granma is not here to say "We got no business over there!"

But I hear her anyway.

At the Vietnam Veterans Memorial

How quickly the tears come
is a tribute to their valor and to Maya Lin
and the perfection of her vision.

I perform an experiment
for my students back in San Antonio.
Standing before each panel
near the casualty-rich center
I count the seconds
until my eyes find a name
that tells of Indian-Spanish heritage:

    A thousand and one--Flores
    A thousand and two--Gonzalez
    A thousand and three--Zuniga
    A thousand and one--Flores

It is a bad day for flowers
and I cannot exceed three seconds.

    The air cavalry burns another village to save it as
    the choppers clip the morning air over the scent of
    jellied gasoline and the sound of crying children
    the fresh troops fly in and the body bags fly out.

After they pulled down the tipi
an Arapaho elder
raised a trade goods hatchet-pipe
and the young officer who rode him
down
turned to finish the old man
and was almost thrown for
not knowing that a horse
will try not to step on a human being
or not knowing that the elder
struggling to rise on his unbroken arm
was a human being.

Across the grass there is a new monument to the women.
One nurse holds a pressure bandage
on the chest of a fallen warrior
with the heel of her hand
another gazes skyward
for Med Evac.

The smell of powder and the haze it creates and the
constant din-din-din of automatic weapons fire
takes all the senses out of the world but for a
wild shout that cuts through all the overloaded
neural pathways and connects to the here and now:

"Medic! We need a medic!" Women were not supposed
to be battlefield medics, but they forgot to tell
the battlefield.

The young officer ended the
encounter
with a pistol shot to the head
close enough to spatter
the blue coat red.
He had another for the elderly woman
ululating over the body.

The statue raised to placate
those who did not share Maya Lin's vision
is not as dreary as I expected.
Three young warriors, bone-tired,
seem to be regarding
the names of their fallen comrades.
I stand beside them, crying.

Young Warrior

for Paul Russell-White

I told him
     his father told him
go in this order: Air Force
                       Navy
                       Army
                       Marines

So naturally, he went directly to the Marine Corps
recruiter.

When he aced the tests and the recruiter started talking
technical school,

I told him
     his father told him
go in this order: Electronic
                       Administrative
                       Mechanical

So naturally, he told the Marine Corps recruiter "combat
infantry."

When the assignments were made,

I told him
        his father told him
go in this order: Stateside
                                     Europe

So naturally, he volunteered for hazardous duty.

He is not Dragging Canoe, Stand Watie, Ira Hayes or a
Diné Code Talker.

That was then and this is now, and he is my son.

And naturally,

this is how Indian sons have always served the
conqueror:

Semper Fi!

Disruption, Spring 1997

"An Albuquerque school board has refused to
allow an Indian girl to graduate in a traditional shawl
handmade by her grandmother, citing 'disruption' of the
ceremonies. . ."

The speakers droned on in English
and her mind wandered.

She caressed the bundle absentmindedly
as if to stroke one last time
the cloth she had labored over for so many nights
after cleaning the rooms at the motel.

She smiled at her cleverness.
She had taken the silver concho belt
that had belonged to her man and his father before.
Having no male children or grandchildren
she let the trader
cut it to fit a woman's waist,
leaving some room
for the fullness to come in the years beyond eighteen.

Her man had been large,
from a clan of large men,
and the excess silver from his belt
bought the fine cloth and bright threads
and her fingers did the rest.

It was not her tribal custom
to speak the names of the dead
but she saw in her mind's eye
his smiling face
shining with pride in his granddaughter
and pride in his wife.

Jolted to attention
by the calling of her granddaughter's English name,
she moved like a dark shadow
through the white throng
clutching the contraband to her chest with both hands
and as the dark-eyed Indian girl stepped from the stage
the grandmother, greatly daring,
opened the shawl with the bright colors
and the thousands of tiny stitches
and the perfect fringe
and threw it over the shoulders of the girl who stood,
first in her family,
holding her diploma.

The police were called
and order was quickly restored.

Texas Indian History in Ten Haiku

I.
Apacherìa
killed Spanish missionaries,
kept its secrets well.

II.
Coahuiltecan,
Karankawa and Caddo--
extinguished Texans.

III.
Buffalo, bison,
and the Texas Ranger name:
"Comanche larder."

IV.
Tonkawa friendlies
promised reservation here.
Oklahoma bound.

V.
Chief Quanah Parker:
bringer of peyote to
Indian prayers.

VI.
Our Legislature
"out of Indian business"--
poverty persists.

VII.
A minority
too small to elect is not
a minority.

VIII.
We won't disturb graves
belonging to yonega
who return favor.

IX.
Gambling means no
eating commodity cheese,
but serving of brie.

X.
Briefcase warriors
ululating; counting coup;
seeking dignity.

What Indians Want

"What do you want?"
The Question comes
with and without good will
but it comes.

"Acknowledgment of our history here!" says my Indian
sister Ruth Soucy.

"Denazification!" says the faux Indian
Ward Churchill.

These things and more,
and they will cost you dear!
More than giving the country back,
much, much more.

I think of the German civilians forced to file through the
death camps at the point of American guns,
how the civilians tried to turn away
but our GIs grimly insisted
and the German townspeople
stood there and cried, more
naked than the stacks of
naked Jewish corpses,
stripped of deniability.

Once you stand there
naked,
stripped of innocence,
bereft of "Indian depredations,"
without casinos or tax exemptions or smoke shops--
without myth or trivia,

when you stand there
naked as my hunger,
when you know the price
of taking a deer
without the deer's permission,

then we can talk.

Indian Lawyer's Creed

I am an Indian lawyer, a briefcase warrior. I stand between Indian people and those who would do them harm. The warrior's role is a duty and an honor.

I defend the few resources that have not been taken from us so Indian people may survive.

I defend the land and air and water on and off reservations so all people may learn to live in harmony with the Creator's work.

I defend the right of Indian people to govern themselves, worship as they choose, and return their dead to the earth.

I will not use my skills against Indian people no matter how wrong I believe them to be. We suffer enough without causing each other to suffer.

I will not use unethical methods in the practice of law because that would dishonor the people I represent.

I will not accept fees from Indian people beyond my needs. If I receive fees from other people beyond my needs, I will remember that a wealthy Indian is one who can quickly forget duty and honor.

Whether I practice or teach or hold office, I will always remember the duty of an elder to share knowledge with young men and women who aspire to be warriors.

I am an Indian lawyer, a briefcase warrior. I stand between Indian people and those who would do them harm. When I do this, I bring honor to my tribe, my clan, and myself.

On Reading Oda a Unas Flores Amarillas

December has come.
But through the white blanket of doom and shambles
poems like flowers beckon,
and as great grey machines
clangor in the freezing mist
--pink-tinted snow lying in Santiago's streets--
here and there
small yellow flowers
persist with stubborn vengence.

1974

Haiku for Walela

Wings of silken thread

shining time unmeasured'

beats invisible.

Not Juan Valdez

In Chiapas,
a man rises and pulls on plain white garments
scrubbed from the river
    En Chiapas se levanta un hombre
    y se pone su ropa sencilla blanca
    lavada en el río
takes bandana and straw hat, a long drink of water,
and heads to work before the sun
    toma su pañuelo y sombrero de paja
    un trago grande de agua
    y se va a trabajar antés que salga el sol
stopping at the Catholic mission
and again at a private place
to thank all gods that will listen
that his children are healthy.
    parando en la misión Católica
    y tambièn en un lugar retirado
    a darle gracias a cualquier diós que escucha
    por la salud de sus hijos.

The green coffee beans flying through his nimble fingers
into canvas sacks
are stained by the steam from the humid plants
mixed with his sweat
and we know
that his name is not Juan Valdez.
    Los frijoles verdes de café
    pasando por sus dedos ágiles
    a sacos de lona
    contienen el vapor de plantas humedas
    mezclado con sudor
    y sabemos que él
    no se llama Juan Valdez.

In Seattle,
a man in Polo and Nike and Ralph Lauren
    En Seattle
    un hombre vestido de Polo, Nike, Ralph Lauren
sips Chiapas coffee,
    bebe a sorbitos su café de Chiapas

barely touches his croissant and kiwi
        Muy poco come de su pan y kiwi
notes on the front of the international section
that Indians are being killed in Chiapas,
        Lee en frente de la sección internacional
        Que matan indígenas en Chiapas
wonders briefly what they have done to provoke this
turns to the business section
to check his portfolio
        Se pregunta de pasada
        que habrán hecho para merecer esto
        va a la sección de negocios
        para revisar sus valores
congratulates himself for remembering
to have his secretary pick up something
for his daughter's birthday,
        se felicita porque se acordó
        decirle a su secretaria
        que le traiga algo para su hija
        que cumple año
waves down the waitress to refill his coffee
        llama a la mecera que le dé más café
        y él tampoco se llama Juan Valdez.
and his name is not Juan Valdez, either.

Chitto Harjo

Crazy Snake said: "Don't sign!"
    Indians signed.

Crazy Snake said: "Hold the white man to his
word!"****
    Indians took what they could get.

Crazy Snake refused his allotment. They put him in a
cage.

> **** "He told me that as long as the sun shone and the sky is
> up yonder this agreement will be kept. He said as long
> as the sun rises it shall last; as long as the waters run it
> shall last; as long as grass grows it shall last. That is
> what he said, and we believed it."

(Indian justice under white rule required only a whipping
post and a gallows: whipping and death, pain and the
end of pain. A couple of cells to sober up drunks--but no
living in a cage.)

They put Crazy Snake in a cage. Almost everybody signed, and the Muscogee Reservation disappeared.

Leaving historians to examine the transaction and ask:

Who was crazy?

Who was a snake?

The Year They Drilled for Oil

Ten months before the lease was up
they brought in the drilling rig.

The driller's shack took the bean field.

Joe tried to put in some lettuce around the edges
but those big tires don't know
lettuce from Bermuda.

There was not enough Bermuda left to graze the cow,
so Joe's kids learned to get milk in bottles.

The hole killed one of the roots on Joe's pear tree.
It didn't die, but there were no pears that year.

The noise from the rig disturbed the chickens
and they quit laying.

One morning we found the beehive empty,
and we all helped put up the honey in jars,
not knowing when there would be more.

The pond down below the well got salty and all of Joe's
catfish died at once.

We were afraid to eat the fish, but Joe said we could use
them to fertilize the corn.
The corn came that year
in small ears
with tiny hard kernels
that did not gush juice
across the table
when bitten.

Only the melons
seemed to ignore the drilling,
but when the fruit came
it tasted salty, like chemicals.

The blackberry bushes along the fence line
were coated with dirt,
and the berries had to be washed with care
but we got a few pies.

The man from the oil company came to see Joe in the last
month of the lease and said the rig would have to leave
soon.

Joe, a six foot Muscogee who called himself "Red Stick
Creek," started to cry.

Not understanding, the oil man offered to stay and bring in the well if Joe would extend the lease on terms a bit more favorable to the company. He said the core samples looked "very promising."

Joe declined.

I heard the oil man tell another as they walked away that Joe had missed a chance "better than nothing."

"These Indians," he said, "just do not understand how to use land."

Next year, the pear crop was small, but it came early.

Eleven Mile Hill

There's a hill outside Austin
where 35 pulls its weary pilgrims
up from San Antonio.

Top it at night, northbound
and find yourself astride the world of Austin
above decades of lights.

Did the Comanche fires ever show this far away?
tiny flickering vagrant dots on an immense blackness
telling stories did the Comanches?
around star mirrored fires
while the Spanish huddled behind the adobe
of San Antonio de Bexar
and killed the tame Indians with disease?
before decades of lights.

Did the gas lights of Waterloo show themselves eleven
miles away?
Did Comanche riders look down on the fires that burned
no bison chips?
and wonder whether the bison had a place?
among decades of lights.

45

Do the Wendlerville lights still spread in regular
rectangles
and graceful curves
to banish the empty blackness
of warm Texas nights
unlit by the stars?

Could an avenging golden-cheeked warbler called by
long dead undead Comanches unplug them one by one?
and diminish
        blinking out
and diminish
        square by square
and diminish
        make the land younger

decades of lights?

Bison Bones

Were Dallas Texans born with neckties on
to be served in deep carpet
by smiling brown faces
where dishes disappear silently
and condiments come in tiny sealed jars
to dine on bison bones?

Would a Texas--Comanche killer--Ranger
look askance,
dusty duster flapping in the air conditioning,
horse--Comanche wealth--at the curb,
shrug in amusement and sit down
to dine on bison bones?

Would a barefoot Yaqui vaquero
from South Texas cow country
where stands of mesquite--Indé food--trees
are strangled by heavy chain
pulled taut by bulldozers
smile as his brown callused feet
sink deeply in the carpet that knows no crumbs
smile secretly and sit
to dine on bison bones?

A suit greets a suit
at the next table.
"How are yew?" wife's skirt rustles silently as she bends
for an insincere hug
and I wonder if her heels rise toward the ceiling
as the white blanco blanco blanco legs
of her chosen suit
squirm between her own
for surely a man must have great cojones in his pants
to sit in downtown Dallas
and dine on bison bones.

Dallas. September 27, 1994

The Business of the Sea

Land bound on the Third Coast,
fresh morning deep breathing and far gazing
hair in wind mind at rest heart at sea.

Barges and trawlers
a sterile distant disturbance

going about the business of the sea.

Shrimpers and their seabird escort
bisect a horizon
      sea colored and sky painted
      sky colored and sea painted
advance guard for
            fragile tankers
            bulging freighters
            sleek warships

going about the business of the sea.

Land bound and looking less organized
than pounding diesel purpose
devoid of metal
innocent of internal combustion
wandering from pregnancy to birth,
gravid with random life:

> sea turtles lumbering ashore to bury their eggs,
> Friday's tracks on a virgin beach,
>
> sandpipers tricky-tracking tiny prints in wet sand,
> feeding daintily,
>
> gulls,
> rowdy and raucous,
> scolding and demanding,
> another conspiracy of flesh, feathers and bone,

going about the business of the sea.

For Dennis Brutus

The police wait, not unkindly,
servants of the open guarding lackeys of the closed. . .
They wait in good humor to catch the birds flown against
the window
       drawn by the reflection of fire and steel
       children of presidents, would-be presidents, even
       of King
       beating blindly against the glass
       drawn by the reflection of fire and steel
The police wait, without malice, for the polite rituals of
defiance.
They wait and listen to the soft thump of feathered bodies
drumming like sentient rain
       of death
       of torture
       of dreams denied (deferral being a politically
       untenable position)
The police wait, black and white together, to defend the
indefensible. They wait to do their duty, to gather up the
bodies of small birds beaten against the glass, drawn by
the reflection of fire and steel.

REPUBLIC OF SOUTH AFRICA EMBASSY
WASHINGTON, D.C.
1985

51

Jailpoem 2

Four cold steel grey walls
Three long hours
or two
or maybe they don't allow time here.

Tantalizing talisman-keys jangle past
echo pounding doors. . .
(Oh God,
come for me this time! For me!)

Who saw me go down?
Amid the gas,
maybe none
or perhaps they don't allow friendship here.

Formulating resistance plans, passing time
(or what
passes for time
in this grey-walled limbo of fear).

In the repentant stillness, I do not repent.

1970

Honor Rap

Heathens need to hear the Word
and Brutus is an honorable man.
Indian land use is absurd
and Brutus is an honorable man.

The treaty's good while rivers run
and Brutus is an honorable man.
Ink gets dry; the theft's begun
and Brutus is an honorable man.

Women and kids have to die
and Brutus is an honorable man.
Nits make lice and elders cry
and Brutus is an honorable man.

Indian digging is a game
and Brutus is an honorable man.
To save his bones, know his name,
and Brutus is an honorable man.

Et tu, Bruté? Doin' your job?
Murder by the cops
and law by the mob,
white man's corn and red man's cob,
but Brutus is an honorable man.

Dreaming

I could not tell if I was dreaming.

You know how it is. You wake up but something about reality doesn't seem quite right and you think you might still be asleep but you can't really tell?

I stumbled out of bed and started the coffee machine burbling and collected the newspaper from the front yard.

The sports page told me that the New Jersey Niggers had beaten the Boston Micks.

Some player on the Houston Hebes had accused the San Antonio Spics of dropping their last game to get a higher draft pick.

The league was expanding to Toronto, and since they had already honored African-Americans, Irish-Americans, Jewish-Americans and Hispanic-Americans, they wanted to name a team to honor Native Americans.

They sent out notices to all the tribal leaders, and they told us we could have whatever we wanted: Prairie Niggers, if the New Jersey team did not object, Redskins, Savages, Warriors, Heathens, Braves, Bucks--and of course the cheerleaders would be the Squaws, unless we wanted to modernize the language and just call them the Cunts.

But the tribal leaders voted for a write-in candidate, the Treaties.

"Toronto Treaties." It has a nice ring to it.

But the league was puzzled. What kind of a name is that?

"If the United States and Canada want to honor the First Nations," said the tribal leaders, "honor our treaties."

And there was a sidebar story. It seems that the President of the United States and the Prime Minister of Canada had heard this and called a joint press conference.

"We had no idea," they said, "that our countries have violated so many agreements with Native Americans. We have formed a joint commission to recommend how to make it up to the survivors, and we have each proposed legislation tendering a formal apology."

And it was at that moment I knew I was dreaming.

A Matter of Faith

A golden eagle in the Sandias
returned my camera's gaze fearlessly.
She knew her beauty
like a graceful woman contained in herself.

> Bless this long Japanese lens this cloudless day
> this proud bird!

Eagles are sacred because they ride the wind to the place
of the spirits and they can share what they learn of that
misty distant place if they choose. We believe this but
because we cannot ride the eagle to the place of the
spirits it becomes a matter of faith.

On the way down from the Sandias
the camera told me 36 but stuck at 26.
Stubbornly, I cocked the lever with my clumsy thumb,
beat the film until it quit resisting
having been torn from the end of the spool.

A golden eagle in the Sandias
possessed my camera and was possessed.
She knew her beauty
like a graceful woman contained in herself.

These moments are sacred because sometimes an eagle will share its knowledge with a human being. I believe this but because I destroyed my film you cannot ride it to the place of the eagles and so

it becomes a matter of faith.

Sisters Three

A place to safely be
has to please the sisters three.
      Go to water,
       search the sky,
stand with two fists full
of your mother's body
and ask.

An elder woman's blood
sacred to all Cherokee:
      Go to water,
       watch the sky,
and ask for Selu.

The harder woman's heart
gives up life with passion's fire:
      Go to water,
       watch the sky,
and ask for Toya.

To count the young one yours
dries her love before her years:
      Go to water,
       watch the sky,
and ask for Squasi.

Repatriation

We found a little yellow bird
-singing the land
from a tree covered hillside-
that might be a golden-cheeked warbler
but maybe not
because few are left these days
and it's hard to tell
but we let him stay
because he is beautiful
and he can sing.

We found some whitened bones
poking through the soil
near the swimming hole
where the water runs sweet and clean and cold
-except when they water the golf course.

We met a frail old man in jeans and a flannel shirt
-lines in his face sculpted from red clay,
who smelled of tobacco and sang
words without meaning
to owners of land-
who might be a Comanche medicine man
but maybe not
because few are left these days
and it's hard to tell
but we let him bury the bones
because he is beautiful
and he can sing

"Indian America"

Oklahoma of Rogers and Hammerstein
     and green growing lilacs
     hard by red dirt roads and paintless outhouses,

Oklahoma of Will Rogers the Paint Clan Cherokee
     with the friendly grin
     and wit like a straight edge razor,

Oklahoma of the Deep Fork bottom
     and papershell pecans,
     whiskered catfish,
     3.2 beer and holy rollers,

Oklahoma of Friday night football,
     rodeo cowboys,
     and niggertown Saturday night,
Oklahoma of bootlegger pints
     and small town vandals,
         Indian art,
         Indian clothing,
         Indian food,
         Indian Indians in Indian America
         where an Indian can be anything

except alive.

What I Learned and Didn't Learn at the Bristow,
Oklahoma Historical Society Museum

I.

Peanuts grow without dirty hands.

Oil wells drill themselves.

Oklahoma was empty land, settled by people in neckties
who were served by invisible cooks and waitresses.

Slavery and Jim Crow left no mark in the red dirt of
Oklahoma. The Historical Society removed the
"Colored" restrooms and water fountain to be certain of
that.

Oklahoma was a land without Negroes, Indians,
roughnecks, drunks, whores….

A land where crops and goods appeared and swell people
traded among themselves between church services on
Sunday and Wednesday and football games on Friday.

It was such a perfect place—no wonder I had to leave.

II.

When Gene Autry worked at the Frisco Depot

The Frisco Depot had four restrooms and two water
fountains

When Gene Autry worked at the Frisco Depot

Henry Dawes had so recently stolen the Muscogee
Nation

that the owners still smoldered and sought out the

bootleggers

When Gene Autry worked at the Frisco Depot

Halliburton was North of town

Bristow was peanut farms and oil wells

Gene Autry went to Hollywood

Halliburton to Iraq

The peanuts moved to Georgia

Not likely to come back

Moneychangers tell the Temple's story

of Gene Autry at the Frisco Depot

Negroes who knew their place

An oil patch without roughnecks

Peanuts grown without hands in the red dirt

Steakhouses where dishes washed themselves

White bankers and bosses in ties and suits with golden

watchfobs

Smugly tread on Muscogee bones.

When I'm Old

And when I am very old

will the drums outrun my feet?

Will the sweetgrass be just another smoke, and the sage a
burning weed?

Does White Buffalo Calf Woman return for the civilized
Indians?

Asked about the White Buffalo, the spiritual leaders of
the Seven Clans
              replied,
              replied simply,
              replied of necessity,
              replied for survival:
       "What is sacred to one is sacred to all."

And when I am very old

will the Cherokee Syllabary cloud my eyes?

Will the stomp dance be the pastime of ghosts,
and the powwow highway just another interstate?

Does Buffalo Calf Woman return for
   the civilized Indians?
   the mixed-bloods?
   the English speakers?
   the clanless lovers?

Can we love who we love? teach our children? bury our
dead?

when I am very old?

Planting

I'll not see this harvest in,

perhaps not hear the green corn welcomed by the drums
again.

I'll plant it just the same,

the dry corn in straight rows,

Selu's gift.

The planting's done

and I wheeze like the summer wind

subdued by the cold northers

just before the harvest.

I believe I'll lie here

between these rows

and rest a bit,

talk to the clouds,

make myself useful.

How to Succeed as an Indian Poet

Don't say "hunger."
Write of the plump red strawberries
grown by Cherokees
in the Cookson Hills,
rather than rodents fried in lard,
garnished with herbs from the bar ditch,
government commodities on the side.

Don't say "homeless."
Write of the red wildflowers and stark beauty
of the Black Hills in South Dakota
rather than the gutted mobile homes and appliance
cartons
on the Pine Ridge Reservation.

Don't say "disease."
Tell us of the red sand
slipping through the hand
of a Navajo medicine man
rather than reminding us
that hantavirus is spread by rats.

Don't say "genocide."
Tell us of Red Cloud and Rolling Thunder,
Crazy Horse and Tecumseh,
safe dead Indians
--Pontiac as a hood ornament--
rather than reminding us
of a Cheyenne child at Sand Creek
exploding like an overripe watermelon,
red within and red without,
from the business end
of a .50 caliber Sharps.

Do tell,
do write,
O wise and noble red man,
Native American shaman,
share your hard won wisdom
---but not too much of it.

Bosque Redondo:
Homage to Yevgeny Yevtushenko

Over Bosque Redondo
there is a new memorial.
Stones from Dinetah on the rolling flat near the brackish
river.

          Today I'm as ancient in years as the
          Diné people.
It seems to me at this moment--
          I am Diné.
Instead of The Trail Where We Cried,
          The Long Walk.
Instead of Tsa-la-gi,
          Diné.

Oh, how you taught us our assigned station!

You taught us well!

Even today, the ladies with parasols

     point with scorn at drunken Indians outside Gallup

bars,

     point as they daintily avoid the New Mexico sun

and search between the bars for old pawn treasures,

     point as another 'skin, pawn money drunk up, is

chucked into the street.

     point at the present without seeing the past, recent

past:

               "Red niggers!"

               "The only good Indians I ever saw

               were dead."

               "Don't play with the Indians, dear."

Oh, my American people!

I know the melting pot is your guiding metaphor.

But those with unclean hands--stained with the blood of people who will not melt--besmirch your own clean name:

the "Indian fighters" and their great battles, their Washitas and Sand Creeks, reputations written with the blood of women and children and old men,

the missionaries who broke our connections and took our souls in exchange for names in Spanish and English,

the Indian agents who stole us blind in both the buying and the selling,

the politicians who say we're extinguished, distant history and garbled fiction, Squanto and Tonto.

The goodness of my native land I know.

But an Indian child, frail as a twig in April, trembles

before your schools.

I want just that we should see each other--as we are.

Here we were forbidden the sacred

journey to the four corners of Dinetah. How can I show

you the rocky spire where Spider Woman gave the gift of

weaving to the Diné? If I cannot, how will you know a

Navajo rug?

Over Bosque Redondo only rustling wild grasses move.

The trees watch sternly

like judges arrayed.

Here silence itself cries aloud--

I remove my hat

and feel I am gradually going gray.

This is no place to take a child to play

until she is ready to hear the story

spoken by this land. When is that, I wonder?

And I myself

am like an endless soundless cry,

over these thousands of buried ones.

Each one

of these murdered elders

am I.

I

am each of their murdered

sons and daughters.

Nothing within me will ever forget this

that nothing outside me dares to remember.

76

Let the drums thunder their might
when will be buried for eternity
the earth's last racist White.

Native blood my veins runs through
but Scottish blood and Irish too
as proof that love crosses between us.

Let the hatred that birthed this place of fear
and the Starving Diné Clan
sink into this sterile soil.

Let the tourists who come upon this ground
that grew nothing but pain
mourn the lives represented by these stones from Dinetah
and come away free, resolved to answer
those who question pedigree: I am a true American!

Made in the USA
Charleston, SC
28 December 2012